COMPOUND INTEREST.

The eighth wonder of the world.

Millionaires secrets.

Divine Mason

TABLE OF CONTENT:

In this book, compound interest, accumulate interest, accumulate dividend, build interest, accumulate revenue and accruing funds are used interchangeably. They simply mean the same thing; **COMPOUND INTEREST!**

CHAPTER 1

INTRODUCTION:

WHAT IS COMPOUND INTEREST?

There are sayings that COMPOUND INTEREST is the 8th wonder in the world.
It is the most powerful weapon that can ever be used financially.
He, who comprehends it, acquires it; he who doesn't, pays it.

Compound interest (or accumulating interest) is the interest on an advance or store determined in light of both the underlying head and the collected interest from past periods.
The rate at which compound interest builds relies upon the recurrence of building, with the end goal that the higher the quantity of accumulating periods, the more noteworthy the self-multiplying dividends. In this manner, compound interest gathered on $1000 compounded at 10% every year will be lower than that on $1000 compounded at 5% semi-yearly throughout a similar time span. Since the interest-on-interest

impact can produce progressively sure returns in view of the underlying chief sum, accumulating has once in a while been alluded to as the "marvel of accruing funds."

BROAD VIEW OF COMPOUND INTEREST:

Compound interest happens when premium gets added to the chief sum contributed or acquired, and afterward the loan cost applies to the new (bigger) head. It's basically interest on interest, which over the long haul prompts remarkable development.

Compounding can actually benefit you as your reserve funds and ventures develop over the long run or against you assuming that you're taking care of obligation. Peruse on for additional with regards to what accumulating funds works and how it can mean for your accounts.
While accumulate interest is ostensibly the main part to establishing financial stability, it can likewise be perhaps the most ideal way to wreck your funds: Having to pay build interest can make obligation twisting crazy.

A great many people just consider revenue as far as how high or low a rate is. Yet, seeing how interest is determined, or builds, is significant as well. Realizing how compound interest functions can assist you with staying away from costly missteps and take advantage of your cash, regardless of whether you're keeping it, contributing it, acquiring it, or spending it.

CHAPTER 2

THE HISTORY OF COMPOUND INTEREST:

It is by and large concurred that the beginning of compound interest can be followed back to the Old Babylonian time frame (ca. 2000-1600 BCE), on the grounds that we realize that the Babylonians called build interest şibāt şibtim "interest on interest" in Akkadian, and, surprisingly, tackled numerical issues on it.

Compounding interest when charged by moneylenders was once viewed as the most terrible sort of usury and was seriously censured by Roman regulation and the normal laws of numerous different nations.
Remembered to have begun in seventeenth century Italy, accumulate revenue can be considered "interest on interest," and will cause a total to develop at a quicker rate than simple interest, which is determined uniquely on the chief sum.
Compound interest made horticulture conceivable and turned into a significant piece of people framing urban areas. The beginning of revenue goes before the improvement of cash. Credits of

seeds and creatures were logical the earliest types of interest. Seeds yielded increments, and after a gather they could be gotten back with interest.

CHAPTER 3

ADVANTAGE OF COMPOUND INTEREST:

* Compound interest makes your abundance become quicker.

* It makes an amount of cash develop at a quicker rate than straightforward premium since you will bring in returns on the cash you contribute, as well as on returns toward the finish of each building period. This implies that you don't need to take care of as much cash to arrive at your objectives!

* Compound interest will be "interest paid on the interest" and this is the significant force of self-multiplying dividends.

* The additional time, the more development potential: The bigger your beginning sum and the bigger your return, the quicker your investment funds compound. Also after some time, it can truly add up. Saving early and frequently can place the influence of compound development in support of yourself by giving your cash something to do so you don't need to!

DISADVANTAGES OF COMPOUND INTEREST:

One setback of accumulate interest is that it makes debt (student loans, mortgage, credit card etc.) develop speedier and all the more significantly after some time.

Another disadvantage of exploiting compound interest choices is that it can some of the time be more costly than you understand. The expense of accumulate interest isn't in every case promptly obvious and in the event that you don't deal with your venture intently, creating revenue installments can really lose you cash.

One more disadvantage to accumulate interest is that its advantages apply to financial associations and buyers. Moneylenders and credit card backers can apply build revenue to the reimbursement of educational loans and Visa obligation. This interest can outgrow command after some time, particularly for shoppers paying the base month to month sum on these bills.

CHAPTER 4:

HOW COMPOUND INTEREST WORKS:

(How to build wealth with compound interest):

Compound interest is determined by multiplying the underlying chief sum by one and adding the interest rate to the power of the accumulation period minus one. The absolute starting measure of the advance is then deducted from the subsequent worth.
Compound interest works in the accompanying way;

1. Deposit cash in an account:

A store into a ledger or speculation account, for example, a high return bank account, currency market accounts, or a zero-coupon security, can create accumulate revenue. Financial exchange ventures can likewise acquire build interest on the off chance that they deliver profits.

2. Your deposited cash produces interest:

The deposit will produce revenue, which is frequently gathered at a yearly rate. For instance, a store of 1000dollars into a yearly intensified investment account with a 5 percent APY will bring about a total of 1050dollars before the finish of the principal year.

3. The produced interest is compounded:

The APY produces interest on both the chief sum and interest sum from the main year. In light of the past model, the all-out interest would be $52.50. Before the second's over year, the aggregate sum is $1,102.50.

CHAPTER 5

CALCULATING COMPOUND INTEREST:

There are multiple ways for calculation of compound interest:

1. THE COMPOUND INTEREST ALMIGHTY FORMULA:

You can utilize a few numerical approaches to compute compound interest. One of the most direct equations for interest computation is...

A = (PV(1+i)n - P.

In this situation,
"A" is the last sum
"PV" is the current worth of the chief sum
The **"I"** is the financing cost communicated as a decimal rate
"n" is the times the premium will build.

To settle the premium estimation, add one to the loan cost rate, increase the new rate by the time allotment and duplicate that sum by the current worth to get the yearly return. Take away the yearly return from the head to decide the progressive accrual rate.

2. THE COMPOUND INTEREST CALCULATOR:

Numerous calculators both hand-held models and PC programs, have example works that can assist you with computing compound interest rates. There are additionally free web-based number crunchers, including one worked by the U.S. Protections and Exchange Commission.

3. THE SPREADSHEET APPROACH:

Some spreadsheet applications ordinarily include a future worth computation work that financial backers can use to ascertain compound interest. The future worth is the financial worth of an aggregate sometime in the not too distant future, which can determine the future worth of the essential venture in light of gathered interest and interest installments.

4. THE RULE OF 72:

The rule of 72 is a straightforward equation that you can use to decide the quantity of years expected to twofold an investment by dividing the yearly interest rate by 72. For instance; Assuming that the pace of return is five percent, an investment will twofold in around 14 years (72/5 = 14.4).

CHAPTER 6

MAJOR COMPOUND INTEREST INVESTMENTS TO BOOST SAVINGS:

Compound interest speculations are bank-type or currency market resources that build over the long haul. It's the cycle which a resource's income (from capital gains or premium) are reinvested to create more cash. Basically, resources bring in cash, and that cash is returned to for a greater long haul payout.

Funds are determined with the underlying speculation, and the collects reserves. Rather than acquiring assets from straight development, it alludes to the expanding worth of a resource because of the interest of the head and aggregated interest. Along these lines, when your venture develops, it mixtures and acquires more capital for your savings. These ventures can be present moment or long haul, and relying upon how dangerous you need to get, you can get a good profit from your speculation. The following are seven accumulating funds speculations that can help your investment funds.

1. Certificate of deposits:

Considered a protected speculation, Certificate of deposits, are given by banks and for the most part offer higher premium than investment funds. These are governmentally safeguarded time deposit. These CDs pay you interest at customary stretches. As they mature, you get both the head and the interest. Your cash is restricted in these CDs until your record arrives at development, however on the off chance that you needn't bother with the pay immediately, these are a protected venture.

2. High interest savings account:

A high interest/high-return bank account is a wise venture for the people who need cash rapidly. While they might cost a touch more than different speculations, they acquire a higher loan fee that makes it worth the additional cash. With a high interest bank account, proprietors bring in revenue on their cash in view of their stores. Add cash, gain revenue, and most records have a serious financing cost. While you risk expansion, these speculations are okay.

3. Rental properties:

Investment properties are an incredible method for pulling in automated revenue. On disadvantage of this speculation is that as the owner, you need to manage/care for the asset. Properties should be kept up with, and there's no cash to be had in the event that your rental isn't filled.

If you have a client that you can rely on and properties well cared for, rental homes can pull in astounding easy revenue. This investment isn't so free as some others investments listed, assuming you pay down the home loan, this resource can get long haul and consistent income.

4. Bonds:

Bonds can make a great accruing funds venture, yet before you proceed to purchase up a ton, realize that there are various securities with differing hazard factors. Government bonds are the least gamble, and they are supported by the U.S. government. It's dependent upon the fluctuating economy, yet it has liquidity and can be extremely advantageous.

Utility bonds are given by the state and convey somewhat more unsafe than Government bonds. These are upheld by urban communities and states and are dependent on the districts you get them from. Momentary corporate securities have the most elevated hazard. They likewise have the most elevated reward. They are supported simply by the enterprise and are transient speculations. It's impossible to tell what will happen in a year. Be careful of your choice, and your record can benefit.

5. Shares/Bonds:

Rather than playing the security market or bonds, you could take a shot at stocks. To get more out of your corporate shares, profit paying stocks have an extra payout. Obviously, you should choose your stocks admirably. Assuming you pick some unacceptable stocks, you will not get that profit support you need.

You can likewise go with favored stocks. These aren't exchanged as frequently as customary investment opportunities and once more, is completely founded on the stocks you select.

Assuming you are discerning of the securities exchange, this resource might be ideal for you.

6. Real estate investment trust (REITs)

7. Treasury bills

CHAPTER 7

DIFFERENCES BETWEEN SIMPLE INTEREST AND COMPOUND INTEREST:

The distinction between compound interest and simple interest lies in the manner by which the interest is produced. Simple interest is determined every year, founded uniquely on the advance or obligation chief sum, and normally applies to contracts, individual advances, or charge card adjusts.

Borrowers benefit from simple interest since they are just paying interest charges on the head. Financial backers benefit more from build revenue since it can assist their underlying speculation with developing north of quite a while.

CHAPTER 8

SCHEDULES OF COMPOUND INTEREST:

Interest can be accumulated on some random recurrence plan, from day by day to yearly. There are standard intensifying recurrence plans that are generally applied to monetary instruments.

The normally involved intensifying timetable for investment accounts at banks is every day. For certificate of deposit (CD), commonplace intensifying recurrence plans are day by day, month to month, or semiannually; for currency market accounts, it's not unexpected every day. For home equity loans, home mortgage loan, personal business loans, or credit card accounts regularly applied intensifying timetable is month to month.

There can likewise be varieties in the time period in which the accumulated interest is really credited to the current equilibrium. Premium on a record might be accumulated every day except just credited month to month. It is just when the premium is really attributed, or added to the current equilibrium, that it starts to procure extra revenue in the record.

A few banks additionally offer something many refer to as persistently compounding interest, which adds revenue to the head at each conceivable moment. For commonsense purposes, it doesn't gather significantly more than every day building revenue except if you need to place cash in and take it out that very day.

More continuous compounding of interest is gainful to the financial backer or leaser. For a borrower, the inverse is valid.

Compounding/Accumulating periods:
While ascertaining compound interest, the quantity of accumulating periods has a huge effect. The essential rule is that the higher the quantity of compounding periods, the more the compound interest.

CONCLUSION:

More continuous compounding of interest is gainful to the financial backer or leaser. For a borrower, the inverse is valid.

While ascertaining compound interest, the quantity of accumulating periods has a huge effect. The essential rule is that the higher the quantity of compounding periods, the more the compound interest.
Understanding the time worth of cash and the dramatic development made by compounding is fundamental for financial backers hoping to streamline their pay and abundance allotment.

RECOMMENDED BOOKS FROM THE AUTHOR:

1. NFT 1O1
2. 3 EASIEST WAY TO BUILD WEALTH

www.ingramcontent.com/pod-product-compliance
Ingram Content Group UK Ltd.
Pitfield, Milton Keynes, MK11 3LW, UK
UKHW022008190726
13853UKWH00004B/1808